Chá

G000079792

and Even Greater Put-Downs

Jamien Bailey

www.booksbyboxer.com

Published in the UK by
Books By Boxer, Leeds, LS13 4BS
© Books By Boxer 2014
All Rights Reserved

ISBN: 9781909732230

All first meetings between a man and a woman (and a man and a man, and a woman and a woman) must start with a few words.

These may be issued with confidence or stuttered out with an embarrassing gush; they may be sincere, nice and uplifting, cheesy, rude, funny, cheeky or quite filthy, depending on the character of the person giving and the person on the receiving end.

What they all have in common is the same as a 50 ton polar bear,

- they break the ice!

And here is a selection of the best, the worst, the most **cringeworthy**, the most **cheesy**, the most **rude**, the most **downright dirty**, and the most **glorious**.

Plus some of the most cutting responses a poor chap should ever have the misfortune to suffer.

In addition there are some chat-up techniques that have been used with varying degrees of success - and failure - by famous womanisers (and manisers!) whose anonymity must be maintained.

They are all there for you to try, or to try and avoid!

Remember, success is always only a few words away and she may throw you out, but there is only you that can 'throw yourself in'!

The Glorious

May I sit here? I will be able to read my book more clearly from the light emanating from the radiance of your beauty.

You're far too good for me.
Could you just lower your standards for one night, let me dance with you, buy you a drink and see how things progress?

You are a rare individual to possess the gifts of beauty and intelligence, and to carry both with such modesty.

There may or may not be a god, but now I think I believe in angels.

Some girls have it. Some don't. You've got it.

Your eyes are pools of diamonds that reflect the stars, a crystal maze where a man could lose his way and not ever wish to be found.

You are so cute. You must get told this every day.

But I think your beauty is captured within the stars in your eyes, the laughter lines upon your magnificent face and the way your cheeks wrinkle as you smile...

bet you don't get told that every day!

What do you do when you're not dancing/drinking/eating here?

You look like someone who leads an interesting life.

The Glorious

Those shoes/dress/earrings/your hair — looks fabulous. It's probably not just the (clothes) but the way you wear them.

-☆-

Don't you have to be back in heaven before midnight?

-☆-

Did it hurt when you fell out of heaven?

**OK. Enough of that.
Let's move on to the...**

There's alcohol, caffeine and H_2O
on the table.

Do you think there's chemistry between us?

-☆-

It's not a problem you being on your menstrual
cycle — I'll just follow you home on my scooter.

Can I buy you a drink or do you just want
the money?

Fun & The Cheesy

You've got great fashion sense, but what would really be great on you...

...is me!

- ☆ -

Are you gay? No?

Me neither. Let's have sex.

- ☆ -

Fun & The Cheesy

I've got a magic watch that says you're not wearing underwear.

You are?

I must still be on continental time,
it's an hour fast!

-☆-

Looking good from the outside is fine.
But for me, *happiness is inside you.*

I'd walk two miles, barefoot over broken glass, just to smell the exhaust pipe of the laundry van taking away your dirty underwear.

Do you know what the heaviest polar bear in the world weighs? It's enough to break the ice.

Well. Now that the ice is broken...

I'm suffering from memory loss,
do I come here often?

-☆-

How many drinks do I need to buy you before
you'll think I'm good looking?

-☆-

Your body is like having a steering
wheel down my pants
- it's driving me nuts!

Fun & The Cheesy

Do you like food?

Yes?

Me too. We have so much in common.

What's a nice girl like you doing in a place like this?

...or do you always use the men's toilet?

I want you to have my babies.

They're outside, in the car.

-☆-

I want to have some FUN tonight.
I've got the "F" and the "N", all I need is "U".

(P.S. I've got the C and the K as well!)

-☆-

So you deal with customer queries on the phone?
Do you work in a call girl centre then?

Fun & The Cheesy

What do you call that wrinkly, orange coloured, dried fruit, a bit bigger than a grape, that's popular at Christmas time?

Date?

How about tomorrow night then?

Hello. My friends call me "Creepy" but you can call me "Mr. Creep" I'm more of a stalker than a talker.

Hi. You are the most beautiful
woman I've seen...

in the last 30 minutes.

-☆-

I'm attracted to girls who are not conventionally
good looking, in fact, the ones who are plain ugly...

so I'll have to make an exception. In your case as
you are exceptionally, very good looking.

Hi. It's your lucky day. My girlfriend dumped me last night so I'm fresh on the market.

I wish girls would like me for myself and not just for my money.

Your dress is fantastic and, it matches my bedroom carpet.

You: Hi.
She: Hi.
You: Hi, again.
She: Hi.
You: Hi, again.
She: Why?
You: You've got nice Hi's.

-☆-

I think I should take your temperature because
you're hot and cool at the
same time.

I'm a pirate and I've come for your body. Someone
will have to buy me a drink before
I release you.

Do you believe in love at first sight, or should I
come back again — with a glass of champagne?

Apart from being beautiful, what else
do you do good?

Fun & The Cheesy

Shall we talk, or continue flirting from a distance?

-☆-

Don't go yet, you've forgotten something.
What?
Me!

-☆-

Do you believe in helping the homeless?
If yes, take me home with you.

Do you have any Irish in you?
(if no)

Would you like some?
(if yes)
Want some more?

-☆-

Do you mind if I stare at you up close instead of
from across the room?

-☆-

Just so you don't feel bad in the morning after
sleeping with me, I won't wake
you until the afternoon.

I seem to have lost my number...
can I have yours instead?

-☆-

Is it hot in here or is it just you?

-☆-

I have had a really bad day and it always
makes me feel better to see a pretty
girl smile.

So, would you smile for me?

There must be something wrong with my eyes,

- I can't take them off you.

Is there a rainbow, because you're the treasure I've been searching for.

The best thing about you...
would be my arms!

Fun & The Cheesy

I drove you to this lonely spot, on this dark and cloudless night so we could look at the stars and talk about the "hereafter"...

if you're not hereafter what I'm hereafter, you'll be hereafter I'm gone!

You must be rich to afford a boob job and Botox.

Hi, I just wanted to give you the satisfaction of turning me down; go ahead say "no".

"No?"

You don't want the satisfaction of turning me down - let's get engaged.

- ☆ -

I think flat chested girls are more intelligent.

Of course, a book of this type
would not be complete
without including some...

Rude, **Raunchy**
& downright DIRTY

Talk to the hand because the face ain't listening...
but the dick's getting interested!

-☆-

Do you like to dance?

Go dance then, while I talk to your friend.

-☆-

That lump in my trousers doesn't mean I'm pleased
to see you...

it's where I keep my wallet!

I'm only looking at your tits because
I'm too shy to look into your eyes.

-☆-

I'm not a great conversationalist but sit close to me
and something may pop up.

-☆-

Your eyes are the colour of my Ferrari —
red!

A girl like you could help improve
my job prospects —

I'm hoping to move up from *hand* jobs
to *blow* jobs.

-☆-

Are you free tomorrow night? Or will I
have to pay —

like with all my other girlfriends?

What did the mouse with a Porsche
say to the elephant?

You don't need a big willy if you've got
a Porsche.

I've got a Porsche, and I think the mouse
was wrong.

I find the smell of garlic very
refreshing on a girl.

What's the difference between an erection and a Ferrari?

I don't have a Ferrari.

If I said you had a beautiful body... would you punch me in the nuts for being so f*cking corny!

I've got a tattoo down there that says "cupid" on it, but when I look at you it turns into "cut the crap and kiss me stupid."

I don't know which of you ladies has been putting it around that my willy tastes salty.

-☆-

They used to call me 'Donkey Dick' at school,

but I'm a big boy now!

-☆-

I enjoy talking to intelligent people,

but in your case I'll make an exception.

You don't sweat much for a fat lass!

I love astronomy. I'm not exactly Brian Cox but I am interested in checking out Uranus.

I believe women should always be respected.

If you don't believe me, ask that bitch over there that I came in with.

-☆-

You look like an angel that fell from heaven.

Did you get that face when you crashed on the pavement?

-☆-

Do you want to dance?
No?

Then maybe you didn't hear me.
I said you look 'fat in those pants'.

I'm a student gynecologist. I don't know everything, but I'll take a look.

You've got a GOOD LOOK ,

I'm a GOOD COOK

let's go back to mine for a GOOD FU...
...N time together.

**Chat-up Techniques
(with varying degrees of success!)**

**Some to be only tried if
you are desperate!**

Cute Dog

Get a cute dog. There's nothing better as an ice breaker as dogs don't abide by any rules of polite protocol.

He is just as likely to roll on his back inviting a stroke as he would be to sniff her in the crotch, thus initiating a conversation about his embarrassing, uninhibited and naughty behaviour.

Tip: *DO NOT under any circumstances say,*

"Can I do that?"

3 Months To Live

Saying that you've only got 3 months to live to try to get a sympathy shag is desperate in the extreme.

Never a good idea but some get away with it. If you try this, back it up with some medical knowledge and be aware that if you meet the girl/girls after 3 months you might not live for another 3 months.

Tip: *Make sure your mother never finds out.*

Tried & Tested

Something Wrong With My Phone

Tell the girl that there's something wrong with your phone. Ask her to just phone your number to see if it works.

This almost invariably works if you sound convincing enough and then you have the girls number. This does not automatically mean that she won't tell you to piss off and get a life when you ring it.

Tip: *Make sure you get the name right when you phone back.*

£20 Bet

A classic that generally works.

You say:
My friends have bet me that if I come up and talk to you, you'll just send me packing. But if you just smile and let me talk to you for one minute, I'll win £20.

Of course, I would be very happy to share it with you over a couple of drinks.

Tip: *Definitely try this as it has the most likely chance of success.*

Tried & Tested

Share A Taxi

At the taxi rank, offer to share a taxi with an attractive single girl. Hopefully she'll say where she's going and you can say, "that's near enough for me".

If she asks where you are going say, "South, how about you?"

Here you are relying on the fact that most girls have no sense of direction.

Tip: *This can cost you if you go completely in the wrong direction but if your chat is sufficiently good you may be able to go home on the bus in the morning.*

Ice Cube

When you see the girl you want to talk to, have an ice cube ready, put it on the bar or table. Ask if she has anything heavy in her handbag.

Why?

Because I want to break the ice.
The cheesiness of this will get a reaction, hopefully the one you want.

Tip: *Now that the ice is 'broken' keep talking.*

Tried & Tested

Confidence

The most successful chat-up technique is to walk up to the girl and talk with confidence, not easy for many people.

Make strong eye contact and be a little persistent. (Many girls are also equally tongue tied and therefore a certain shyness can be mistaken for reluctance). But don't be too persistent. Try to read the signals. Give compliments and try to be a nice guy rather than a smooth operator.

Tip: *Talk about her favourite subject – herself.*

The Faint

Pretending to faint in front of some attractive female can instantly bring out the nurturing instinct in her. But be careful how you use this and make sure that some big hunky dude doesn't come rushing in to pick you up and make you look frail and stupid.

Explain that this is the first time this has happened and that you'll see a doctor and you'll let her know the outcome, if she is still interested.

Tip: *Don't overdo it or you may end up in hospital!*

Percentages

All the best PUAs (pick up artists) use percentages to get your desired result.

If you only ask 1 girl a month for a date and your percentage success rate is 1 out of 6, that's 2 a year.

Therefore you have to increase your effort.

If you then ask 12 girls in one week, you are going to have more girls than you can probably handle.

Tip: *Warning: This can generate trouble from jealous girlfriends.*

Tried & Tested

Text Speak

On the tube/bus/train, type a text. "What are you listening to?" and show it to the girl next to you. You will have made a move without having to say a word and generally, without having to suffer the pain of a verbal rejection.

The surprise element will usually get a reaction and, if she's a tourist, she'll want to practice her English.

Tip: *Make sure your spelling is not too crap!*

MORE

Downright Dirty

Chat-up lines

What's the difference between an erection and a Ferrari?

I don't have an erection.

But I will have when you're on the bonnet of my Ferrari

- ☆ -

If this conversation goes badly it'll be like the breast implant surgeon using helium instead of silicone...

It will all go 'tits up' !

Your place or mine?

Sorry, it's got to be your place, I'm in a relationship at the moment.

I'm not at all shifty. When I talk to you, I'll look you straight in the tits.

What's the difference between an erection and a Ferrari?

None. I've got both.

I wish girls would like me for myself and not just my money and my big willy.

I believe that if you love someone you should cut them free...

or at least before they pass out!

Remember my name.

You'll be screaming it all night long,
(until you remember the 'safe' word!)

I'd like to screw your brains out,

but it looks like somebody beat me to it.

If we try bondage together, I promise I won't "beat about the bush."

What's the secret of getting into those tight little pants?

Can I start by buying you a drink?

If you come home with me, I'll sleep on the wet patch.

I've got a good gag for you.
I hope you've got a good reflex.

I would love to come across you later.

-☆-

I apologise for coming in my jeans.

If you make me laugh, don't bore me and don't cost me too much money then, in about an hour, I will allow you to take me back to your place, shag my brains out and wake me gently in the morning with a fantastic breakfast.

And if you're really good, I'll allow you to do it all over again tomorrow.

OK. You'll do.

If I could do it all over again...

I'd do it all over you!

-☆-

It's a fact. Men with a large penis often get an itch in their left eye.

(Wink, wink)

-☆-

What speaks French and has a big willy?

Moi!

Great Put-Downs

**The antidote to
a great chat-up line**

♂ You want me to join you?

♀ I think someone should...
you're coming apart at the seams.

-☆-

♂ I want you to have my babies.

♀ Hasn't Social Services already got them?

♂ Most girls think the sun shines out of my ass.

♀ I bet you've got the scorch marks on your underpants to prove it.

-☆-

♂ Where will you be sitting after this dance finishes?

♀ On my arse

-☆-

♂ You look like an angel fallen from heaven.

♀ I wish I'd have fallen on you.

♂ If you were a burger you'd be "McGorgeous", and I'd be , "Mr Whopper".

♀ No.
You'd be Mr. Dinky Winky, Skinny Burger with a Wiener and a gherkin on the side.

-☆-

♂ Yes, you may sit next to me...

but my boyfriend is at the bar and he's got a black belt in GBH.

♂ You remind me of some of my ex girlfriends.

♀ But without the white stick and the labrador?

-☆-

♂ Do you believe in love at first sight?

♀ I might if I saw it.

-☆-

Great Put-Downs

♂ Hey, Darling. Do you f*ck?

♀ I don't – but I do now, you smooth talking bastard!

-☆-

♂ You are very fragrant.

♀ Only 3 months. Does it show.

-☆-

♂ Girls call me "the man who has everything."

♀ Have you tried penicillin?

♂ They call me "Long John Silver".

♀ Is it because you wear long legged
   underpants and don't wash?

♂ You've got 'come to bed' eyes.

♀ You've got 'lock the door, find the pepper
   spray and phone the cops' eyes.

♂ I am an actor, resting after my last job.

♀ Which horror movie was that then?

♂ "You look like someone who is a model or works on aeroplanes."

♀ "You look like someone who works on model aeroplanes."

-☆-

♂ You're out of this world. You must have come from another planet.

♀ You're a UFO – Ugly, Fat & Old.

♂ Talking to you reminds me of my first job, down on the poultry farm, trying to get the chicks into bed at night.

♀ Talking to you reminds me of my first job, down at the fishing bait farm... getting rid of worms that were too full of shit.

Great Put-Downs

♂ How do you like your eggs in the morning?

♀ I don't, I'm a vegan. I prefer squashed nuts.

-☆-

♂ How do you like your eggs in the morning?
♀ Like your brains — scrambled

-☆-

♂ Where have you been all my life?

♀ Hiding from you.

♂ Do you fancy a night out?

♀ Sorry I don't date outside my species.

-☆-

♂ How did you get so beautiful?

♀ I must have been given your share.

-☆-

♂ Hey baby, what's your sign?

♀ No Entry!

♂ If I could see you naked, I'd die happy.

♀ If I saw you naked, I'd die laughing.

♂ Go on, don't be shy. Ask me out.

♀ Okay, get out!

♂ We're like ships in the night.

♀ I'm a Queen Class Liner. You're out of your class — go home for a tug.

♂ Are we dancing?

♀ I wouldn't normally but you've got such a way with words.

♂ Get your coat, you've pulled.

♀ Get a taxi, you haven't!

♂ That dress looks great on you.

♀ It would probably look great on you too.

♂ Your hair colour matches my pillows.

♀ I would have thought that **your** hair colour
would match your pillows...
dirty grey with a touch of grease!

-☆-

♂ Will you go out with me?

♀ I've only just come in!

♂ I've got the body of a god.

♀ Buddha?

-☆-

♂ What's your number?

♀ It's in the phone book.

♂ What's your name?

♀ That's in the phone book as well.

-☆-

♂ You remind me of the last woman who kissed me.

♀ Ugghhh! Your mother!

♂ You remind me of my last date, she was a real doll.

♀ What? A blow up doll?

-☆-

♂ What do you want for breakfast tomorrow? I think you'd like to start the day with a nice sausage inside you!

♀ No thanks. A chipolata wouldn't satisfy my appetite.

♂ I feel magic in the air.

♀ Do you think you could make yourself disappear, then?

♂ Can I dance with you?

♀ Sorry, I'm gay on Friday nights.

♂ We could get real dirty together.

♀ Looks like you've already started.

♂ Could we make a date?

♀ Sorry, I'm washing my hair for the
next six weeks.

-☆-

♂ Have I seen you somewhere before?

♀ No. I never forget a face,
but in your case, I might have made
an exception.

♂ May I see you pretty soon?

♀ Why? Don't you think I'm pretty now?

♂ I think your body is like a temple.

♀ It's only open once a week and today isn't Sunday.

♂ I'd go through anything for you.

♀ Good! Let's start with your bank account.

♂ I would go to the ends of the earth for you.

♀ Yes, but would you stay there?

-☆-

♂ Your place or mine?

♀ Both. You go to yours and I'll go to mine.

-☆-

♂ Have we met before, perhaps once or twice?

♀ Must have been once. I don't make the same mistake twice.

♂ Did I see you here last week?

♀ No. I've never been out before.

♂ I've been on reality TV.

♀ What? On "Britain's Got No Talent"?

♂ What's the chance of me getting you back to my place tonight for a night of sweet passion?

♀ No Chance.
Spelt, "C, H, A, N, C, F, E."

♂ There's no "F" in chance.

♀ Exactly!

♂ Have I seen you somewhere before?

♀ Yes. I'm a nurse at the
Erectile Dysfunction clinic.

♂ You take my breath away.

♀ Good, because I'm finding the whiff of beer
and curry difficult to bear.

♂ Do you come here often?

♀ No. I usually wait until I get home!

Great Put-Downs

♂ What? Go back to your place?

♀ Will there be enough room under that rock
you crawled out from?

-☆-

♂ Have we met before?

♀ Yes. I'm the receptionist at the STD clinic!

-☆-

♂ What do you do for a living?

♀ I'm a female impersonator.

♂ Do you want to know the time?

♀ I'm not going to tell you the time. If I do, we'll get talking. You'll take me home we'll have fantastic sex, so good that you'll want to live with me for the rest of your life. You'll ask me to marry you
- *and I don't want to marry a guy who can't afford a f*cking watch!*

Great Put-Downs

♂ I'd love to get into your pants.

♀ No thanks, there's one asshole in there already.

♂ If I could rearrange the alphabet I'd put U and I together.

♀ If I could rearrange the alphabet I'd put F and U together.

Great Put-Downs

♂ Where have I been all your life?

♀ I wasn't born for most of it.

♂ Haven't I seen you somewhere before?

♀ Yes. That's why I stopped going there.

♂ Can I sit here?

♀ Sorry, Earth's full at the moment,
go back to you own planet.

♂ My place or yours?

♀ Yours. If I'm not there in 2 hours, start without me.

♂ Can I take this seat?

♀ Yes. So long as you take it far enough away.

-☆-

♂ Have I seen you somewhere before?

♀ Probably. I'm a probation officer.

♂ I can give you that 'little bit extra' to all the other guys.

♀ What's that? Chlamydia?

-☆-

♂ I'm SAS.

♀ What? Sad And Stupid?

-☆-

♂ Do you believe in fate? I had a dream about someone exactly like you last night.

♀ Did you get rejected in the dream as well?

Great Put-Downs

♂ I've got my own band.

♀ What type? An elastic one or a gastric one?

-☆-

♂ Do you think I could sit here for
a little while?

♀ Unlikely with your posture.

-☆-

♂ Being here with you is like being in a movie.

♀ Home Alone?

♂ I'll give you £1000 if you let me sleep with you tonight.

♀ Well, I shouldn't really but OK, just the once.

♂ Will you sleep with me for £10?

♀ No. Of course not. What kind of a girl do you think I am?

♂ We've established that. Now we're negotiating over the price.

♂ Are you tired? Because you've been running through my mind.

♀ Not really. There wasn't much else in there to slow me down.

-☆-

♂ Hey babe, your dancing is far out man. You're a real cool chick. What's your sign?

♀ Keep Off The Grass!

♂ When I talk with you it reminds me of some of the great songs of the past.

♀ "Alone, again, naturally?"
"Why does it always rain on me?"

-☆-

♂ What's your sign?

♀ Keep Out - Private Property.

Great Put-Downs

♂ Heaven really is missing an angel.

♀ Well, make sure you're not missing...
the last Handcart for Hell leaves in
about half an hour.

♂ I'm a frog, but if you kiss me I'll turn
into a handsome prince.

♀ In your case that might
take a while.

♂ Do you believe in having sex on a first date?

♀ I don't even believe in a first date.

♂ I had to get drunk to be able to talk to you.

♀ Is that why you're not able to talk to me?

♂ I know how to drive women wild in bed.

   ♀ What, by farting and snoring?

-☆-

♂ I'm shy, can you help me out?

   ♀ Yes. Which way did you come in?

♂ You know what? I'm going to be a star one day.

♀ You can't be Sirius.

♂ I'd love to go out with an older girl.

♀ What for? To help you with your homework?